BUTTERFLIES AND *ALL THINGS SWEET*

THE STORY OF MS B'S CAKES

BY
BONNAE GOKSON

PHOTOGRAPHY
BY
PETRINA TINSLAY
&
A. CHESTER ONG

goff BOOKS

BONNAE GOKSON,
STYLE ICON

BONNAE FIRST APPEARED TO ME *AS WHAT SEEMED LIKE AN APPARITION* – THIS WAS LONG BEFORE WE MADE OUR ACQUAINTANCE. I WAS WALKING ALONG ONE OF THOSE GLASSY BRIDGES IN HONG KONG'S CENTRAL WHEN *SUDDENLY MY ATTENTION WAS DRAWN TO A WOMAN* WHOSE EFFERVESCENT CHARM AND RADIANT CHARISMA SET HER *AGLOW AGAINST* THAT AFTERNOON'S MONSOON *SKY DARK AS CHOCOLATE*. *I WAS COMPLETELY MESMERIZED* BY THIS GREAT BEAUTY IN OUR CITY OF BEAUTIES. BUT IT WAS ONLY AFTER WE WERE INTRODUCED AND *BECAME FAST FRIENDS* THAT I REALIZED *HER TRUE POWER*, AND THE DEPTH OF HER ATTRACTIVENESS. *LIKE THE CAKES SHE CREATES* WITH THEIR GORGEOUS FROSTINGS, BONNAE HAS IMMEDIATE APPEAL, BUT LIKE THEIR RICH FLAVORS, THE *DEPTH OF HER CHARACTER LIES MUCH DEEPER*. **AT THE CORE:** INNATE TALENTS, NATURAL AFFINITY FOR EXCELLENCE, JOIE DE VIVRE. **FOLD IN PLAYFULNESS,** CURIOSITY, HUMILITY, LOYALTY AND HUMOR, AND **SHE IS COMPLETE,** *MADE FROM A RECIPE THAT IS DELICIOUS AND DIVINE*.

CALVIN TSAO, TSAO & MCKOWN ARCHITECTS

In 2012, renowned New York–based architect Calvin Tsao received the Legacy Award from the Museum of Chinese in America (MOCA).

IF THERE WERE AN OSCAR, AN EMMY
AND A GRAMMY FOR THE *BEST LIFESTYLE GURU*
IN THE WORLD TODAY, THEN WITHOUT A DOUBT
BONNAE GOKSON WOULD WIN ALL THREE.

SUZE ORMAN, EMMY AWARD–WINNING PERSONAL FINANCE EXPERT

MANY PEOPLE HAVE STYLE,
AND THEN THERE ARE THOSE RARE,
ONE-OF-A-KIND INDIVIDUALS
WHO SET A STANDARD AND *RAISE THE BAR*
BEYOND OUR *WILDEST EXPECTATIONS.*
I WAS LUCKY ENOUGH TO HAVE ENCOUNTERED ONE OF
THOSE *RARE INDIVIDUALS* WHEN I MET BONNAE
IN HONG KONG MANY YEARS AGO.
EVEN THEN, SHE ENTERTAINED AND CREATED
EVENTS WITH AN *ATTENTION TO DETAIL* THAT
NONE OF US HAD EVER BEEN EXPOSED TO, OR FOR THAT
MATTER EVEN DREAMED OF. WHEN A PERSON
IS *GIFTED* WITH THE ABILITY TO ORCHESTRATE
AN *EXPERIENCE THAT ILLUMINATES* ALL
FIVE SENSES AT ONCE, THAT IS A *CREATIVE GENIUS*,
AND THAT IS BONNAE GOKSON.

KATHY TRAVIS, DIRECTOR OF BRAND INNOVATION, SUZE ORMAN MEDIA INC.

TO BECOME A TRUE STYLE ICON, ONE NEEDS TO
COMMUNICATE AND CREATE WITH ALL FIVE SENSES.
BONNAE IS A FIVE-SENSES STYLE ICON.
SHE MAKES ANY EXPERIENCE OR CREATION A TOTAL
SENSUOUS EXPERIENCE. SHE THINKS ABOUT THE CREATIVE
PROCESS FROM ALL POINTS. SHE HAS A *VISION*
THAT IS SO COMPLETE THAT IT BECOMES
UNFORGETTABLE. SHE WANTS TO BRING *PLEASURE*
TO THE WORLD AROUND HER AND
MAKE EACH MOMENT MEMORABLE
WITH THE POWER OF HER STYLE.

REBECCA MOSES, FASHION DESIGNER AND ARTIST

 *18*

PEONY PETTICOAT
Chiffon,
whipped cream,
mixed berries,
berry mousse

 *25*

FRENCH LACE
Red velvet
and French vanilla
marble cake, rose-petal
and berry jam

 *55*

LADY IN RED
Berry sponge, lychee
cream, raspberry miroir,
macaron

 *57*

SPRING
Strawberry and vanilla
butter cake, pink
Himalayan rock salt

 *82*

MOONSTRUCK'D
Chiffon,
mango and
coconut mousse,
rice crisps, pomelo,
mango glaze

 *86*

ELEANOR
Pandan chiffon,
whipped cream, white
chocolate cornflake
crunch, semi-dried, flaked
and toasted coconut,
sugar orchid

BUTTERFLY KISSES
Rainbow chiffon,
whipped cream, pear
compote, red berries,
peach, kiwifruit,
hand-painted sugar
butterflies

DEATH BY CHOCOLATE
Champagne chocolate
truffle cake,
berry sauce, Swarovski
diamante skull

MONOCHROME
GLAMOUR
Dark chocolate mousse,
white chocolate mousse,
chocolate crisps,
chocolate ganache

GARDEN BEAUTY
Chocolate caramel
chiffon, sugar agave,
sugar fern

DOUBLE HAPPINESS
Crème fraîche
butter cake,
red beans

BE GAGA'D
Chocolate chiffon,
grape jelly, blueberries,
Oreos, chocolate spikes,
silver sugar pearls,
marshmallows

MADAME BUTTERFLY
Beetroot, pistachio
and chocolate chiffon,
apricot compote,
whipped cream,
hand-painted sugar
butterfly

PANSY COUTURE
Chocolate cake,
passionfruit mousse,
chocolate ganache,
sugar pansies

PARADISE
Taro chiffon,
ube cream,
macapuno coconut

PRINCESS
Strawberry crème
fraîche butter cake,
Italian meringue,
jelly beans, gummy bears,
sugar butterflies

WHOOPIE
Red velvet beetroot
cake, cream
cheese frosting,
handmade
licorice allsorts

THE LITTLE PRINCE
Chocolate cake,
Maltesers, French
vanilla crème anglaise,
melted gummy bears

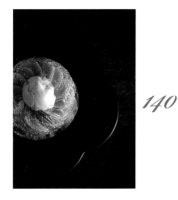

MANGO TANGO
Puff pastry, mango,
mango glaze,
mango ice-cream,
spun sugar

140

EBONY & IVORY
Black sesame and
coconut butter cake,
shredded coconut

146

BETTER THAN SEX
Chocolate fudge cake,
crushed toffee,
caramel crunch,
chocolate wafer crisps,
salted toffee sauce,
sugar lips

155

SCARLET
Marbled vanilla and
red berry Victoria sponge,
sugar camellias

161

MARIE ANTOINETTE'S
CRAVE
Pistachio chiffon,
rose-petal jam, whipped
cream, raspberries,
rainbow macarons,
dragées, cotton candy

185

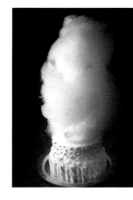

LE LOUIS
Chocolate chiffon,
blackberries, blueberries,
whipped cream,
marshmallows, dragées,
cotton candy

196

CHESTER
French vanilla chiffon,
chestnut purée,
meringue, whipped
cream, Champagne
macarons

200

SUNSHINE
Lemon and poppyseed
chiffon, lemon curd,
whipped cream,
crushed meringue,
sugar poppies

209

SMARTIE PANTS
Chocolate truffle cake,
toffee-covered nuts,
oversize Smarties

227

SEND IN THE CLOWNS
Raspberry and
chocolate butter cake,
old-fashioned
candies, sugar balloons

229

PANSY
Vanilla chiffon,
pineapple bavarois,
fresh pineapple,
sugar pansies

235

LITTLE GEMS
Background: chiffon,
rose jam, raspberries.
Cake stand, upper level:
Sunshine (taster size).
Cake stand, lower level:
pâte à choux, lychee
cream or mango cream.

240

BUTTERFLIES AMAZE ME –
THEIR *BEAUTY*, THEIR *VARIETY*, THEIR *FREEDOM*.
LIKE DREAMS, THEY'RE ALL THE MORE
PRECIOUS BECAUSE THEY DON'T HAVE A LONG LIFE.
THEIR TIME ON EARTH IS FLEETING.

THE **CAKES** I CREATE FOR MY CUSTOMERS
ARE LIKE BUTTERFLIES, *HERE AND THEN GONE*,
DEVOURED IN A FEW SWEET BITES.

THIS BOOK IS THE STORY OF MY CAKES.
IT'S MY THINKING CAP IN A VISUAL FORM.
SPOOLS OF BRIGHTLY COLORED *RIBBONS*,
THE *SEEDS* OF A POMEGRANATE, A FRAGMENT OF
HANDMADE *LACE* THAT HOLDS MEMORIES
OF MY *YEARS IN FASHION*, THE *PETALS* OF A PEONY:
ALL THESE THINGS **INSPIRE ME TO CREATE** CAKES
THAT GIVE PLEASURE TO MY CUSTOMERS.

MY CAKES ARE ALSO THE STORY OF WHAT'S
IMPORTANT TO ME IN MY LIFE.
I VALUE CREATIVITY AND INTEGRITY.
I'M FORTUNATE TO HAVE HAD A LIFETIME
OF EXPOSURE TO *BEAUTIFUL THINGS* ALL OVER THE
GLOBE, FROM **FINE ART TO HIGH FASHION**, AND
NOW CAKES ARE THE MEDIUM IN WHICH **I EXPRESS**
ALL THAT I'VE ABSORBED AND ALL THAT'S
IMPORTANT TO ME.

IT'S AS THOUGH THE CAKE COMES OUT ALIVE;
IT'S AS IF I'VE FOUND MY CALLING. I NEVER EXPECTED IT.
I DON'T EVEN BAKE! BUT TO ME, CAKES ARE
NOT ABOUT MEASURING FLOUR OR SEPARATING EGGS.
EACH CAKE IS A PIECE OF JOY,
A MOMENT OF CELEBRATION.

Bonnae Gokson

TO MY PARENTS, ELEANOR & RAYMOND

WH

PAPER
BONE
PORCELAIN
LINEN
EGGSHELLS
WOOL
PEARLS
LACE
COTTON
ANGELS
STARCH
RICE
COCONUT
IVORY
TAPIOCA
VANILLA
MILK
QUARTZ
SILK
CHIFFON
VIRGINITY
DIAMONDS
BRIDE
MERINGUE
MARBLE
SUGAR
POWDER
CREAM
SALT
SNOWDRIFTS
FROST
ALABASTER
WINTER
INNOCENCE
PURITY
MOONLIGHT
NOBLES
FRESHNESS
CLOUDS
HEAVEN
PEACE
PERFECTION
PEONIES

'White is not a mere absence of color; it is a shining and affirmative thing,
as fierce as red, as definite as black. God paints in many colors; but He never paints so gorgeously,
I had almost said so gaudily, as when He paints in white.'
G.K. CHESTERTON

Peony Petticoat: Chiffon, whipped cream, mixed berries, berry mousse.

———◆———

'I CONSIDER LACE to be one
of the prettiest imitations ever made
of the *fantasy of nature*; lace always
evokes for me those incomparable
designs which the *branches and leaves
of trees embroider across the sky*,
and I do not think that any invention
of the human spirit could have a more
graceful or precise origin.'

COCO CHANEL

———◆———

sugar peony.

French Lace: Red velvet and French vanilla marble cake, rose-petal and berry jam.

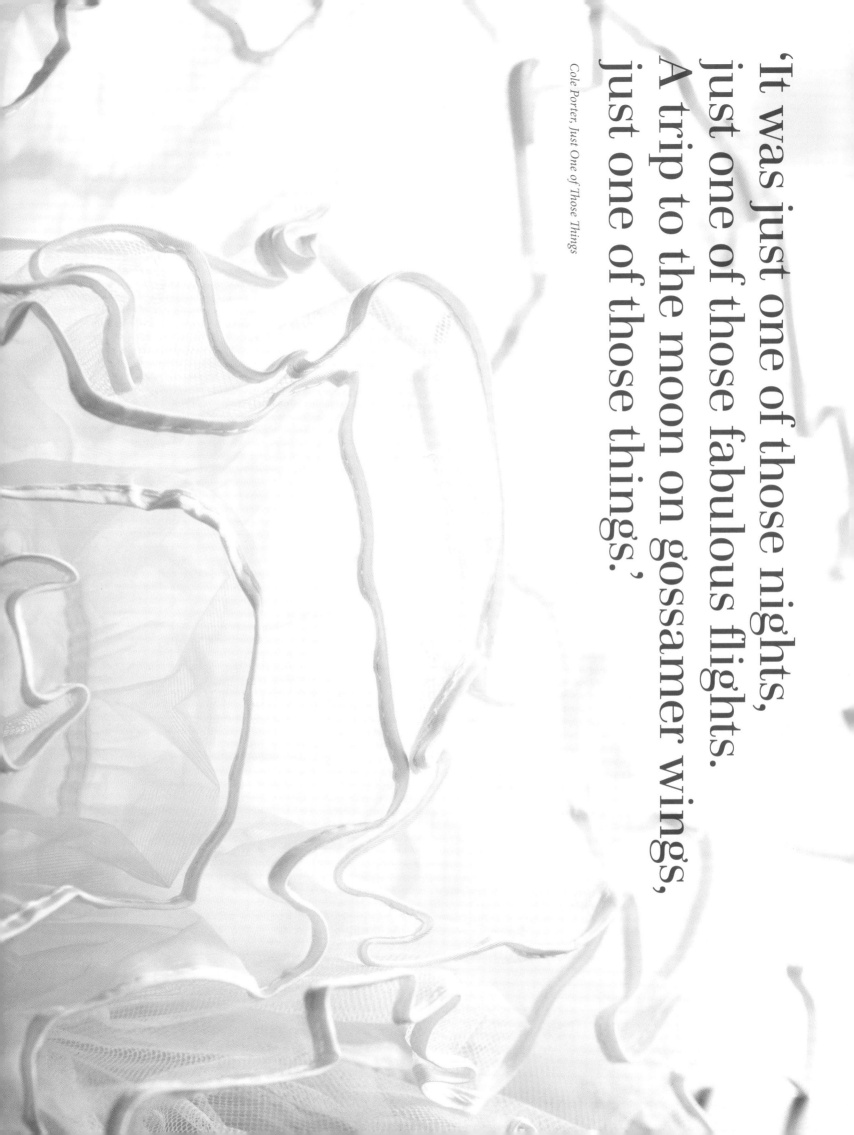

'It was just one of those nights,
just one of those fabulous flights.
A trip to the moon on gossamer wings,
just one of those things.'

Cole Porter, Just One of Those Things

Here Comes the Bride: Rosewater butter cake, jasmine-scented ganache, sugar flowers.

Creating beauty is not effortless. It takes time to build. My inspiration comes from the knowledge and experience I've accumulated in years of working in creative industries, particularly fashion. All my thoughts and memories of working and traveling in Milan, Tokyo, Paris, London, New York, they're all filed, absorbed, ready for me to draw on.

Edgy femininity. Darkness and light. Strength and surrender.

MAGNOLIAS. MANY OF MY CAKES ARE INSPIRED BY NATURE.

Bliss: Pistachio butter cake, almond cream, sugar magnolias.

My mother
gave me these
handmade
cloisonné plates.
A very *refined*
Chinese home
would always
have had
fine tableware
for holding
the wet towels.

I'm the baby of the family by quite some years.
I was Daddy's girl, *and I'll always be a child inside.*

Original Caramel Crunch Cake: Vanilla chiffon, whipped cream, caramel toffee crunch.

The Original Caramel Crunch Cake is my signature, the cake that started it all and made my cakes famous. I created it quite a few years ago for the JOYCE Cafes in Asia.

Opposite: Bird Series No. 6, Qian Gang, oil on canvas, 2012.

The hydrangeas reflect my connection to Australia, where they grow in every yard.
Hydrangeas: Red velvet beetroot cake, cream cheese frosting, sugar hydrangeas.

GARDEN PARTIES

I GREW UP IN A VERY LARGE HOME IN
HONG KONG WHERE WE ALWAYS
HAD *LOTS OF GUESTS*,
SO I'VE HAD A WHOLE LIFETIME OF
LEARNING FROM THE PEOPLE AROUND ME.
I WAS ALWAYS *SEEING AND
EXPERIENCING* THE MOST BEAUTIFUL THINGS,
AND WE WENT TO EUROPE EVERY YEAR
FROM THE TIME I WAS A YOUNG GIRL.
OUTSIDE IN THE GARDENS OF THE FAMILY HOME
WAS A ROUND *MAH-JONG* ROOM.
A MAH-JONG PARTY IS *QUITE AN OCCASION*,
AND IT'S IMPORTANT TO
OFFER A SPECIAL *AFTERNOON TEA*.
THE AMAHS USED TO PREPARE *SANDWICHES* ,
DIM-SUM DELICACIES, **SWEETS AND CAKES**.
YEARS LATER, WHEN I STARTED
SEVVA RESTAURANT, I'D ALREADY LEARNED
THE ART OF ENTERTAINING
FROM MY FAMILY.

THE ART OF HOSPITALITY
I was brought up to understand that when you
go to someone's home, you bring a little gift for them.
When they treat you to dinner,
you handwrite a note to say thank you.
It's a gracious way of doing things, and it's very
strong in Chinese culture. It's about making other
people feel comfortable and welcome.

Lady in Red: Berry sponge, lychee cream, raspberry miroir, macaron.

A MOMENT

My cakes are made to be eaten

while they're very fresh.

They don't contain preservatives.

I'm drawn to the idea of

taking a moment and savoring

that special moment.

You can't go back on it.

When it's finished, it's finished.

Spring: Strawberry and vanilla butter cake, pink Himalayan rock salt.

PSYCHOPHILY:
the pollination of flowers by butterflies.

CROSS-POLLINATION:
the *transfer of ideas* and inspiration between diverse spheres, such as *fashion*, nature, architecture, *visual arts*, graphic design and *pâtisserie.*

Poppies & Stripes: Poppyseed orange butter cake, sugar poppies.

What
about
the men?
They
want
a manly
cake.

I wanted
to create a cake
especially
for my *Chinese
customers.*
To the
Chinese, *gold*
represents
status and wealth.
It's a good omen.

*Million Dollar Truffle Cake: Chocolate truffle ganache, butterscotch-coated walnuts
and hazelnuts, dark chocolate crisps, 24-carat gold leaf, chocolate coins.*

WINTER AT SEVVA.

Dark Chocolate Martini: Valrhona dark chocolate, vodka, crème de menthe, cream, chocolate shavings.
White Chocolate Martini: Valrhona white chocolate, vodka, cream, chocolate shavings.

à toute

Pâtisserie

Festive croquembouche: Pâte à choux, crème pâtissière, toffee, red berries.

We used an embossing technique to create the textured look of the gold fondant for this wedding cake.
I love the way it creates shadows and light and lustre – like a sparkling chandelier.

During the season in October, November and December, I have so many big events, so many weddings, and every bride wants a pink cake. But I didn't want to make another pink cake.

Splendor: Orange and Belgian chocolate cake, sugar peonies.

I love collecting tableware. I bought these Murano glass goblets with semi-precious stones during my travels.

The Moon Festival takes place in autumn,
harvest time, when pomelos are in season and the
moon is large and full, like a pomelo.

Moonstruck'd: Chiffon, mango and coconut mousse, rice crisps, pomelo, mango glaze.

Ah Sung is one of our most highly skilled pastry chefs. His piping work is exquisite.

I created this cake for Mother's Day. It's dedicated to beautiful Eleanor.
Eleanor: Pandan chiffon, whipped cream, white chocolate cornflake crunch, semi-dried,
flaked and toasted coconut, sugar orchid.

Objects of desire: Orchids, of course. And my handmade bone china leaf plate with oversize silver dragées arranged on my friend Alan Chan's design book.

THE ART OF STYLE
MY MOTHER WAS
A VERY *GLAMOROUS WOMAN*,
A *QUEEN* OF FASHION.
I'M NOT TALKING ABOUT STREET FASHION;
I'M TALKING *HIGH FASHION*.
SHE WAS VERY PARTICULAR.
TAILORS CAME TO OUR HOME REGULARLY.
FROM THE TIME I WAS A **LITTLE GIRL**
I WAS *TRAINED* BY THE **WOMEN**
AROUND ME WHO WERE
MUCH OLDER THAN I WAS IN
THE ART OF *STYLE*.

Champagne, Chocolate & Diamonds: Vanilla chiffon, white chocolate mousse, Dom Pérignon Champagne jelly.

CHAMPAGNE, CHOCOLATE & DIAMONDS
I wanted to create something in chocolate, but not dark chocolate. White chocolate.
Something Marilyn Monroe would have loved.
This is the answer, because diamonds are a girl's best friend.

THERE'S NO WRONG TIME TO EAT CAKE. IT DOESN'T HAVE
TO BE A BIRTHDAY CAKE. IT DOESN'T HAVE TO BE AN ANNIVERSARY CAKE.
IT CAN BE A HAVE-A-GOOD-DAY CAKE. WHY NOT?

After I'd styled this cake, my assistant needed to know its name.
I said, 'I can't think of a name right now; please ask me later.'
I walked towards the lift but she was insistent. So I said, 'Okay, let's name it after you.'
And she was very proud. This is the Carmen cake. Very sweet.
Carmen: Dark chocolate chiffon, white chocolate mint cream, baby marshmallows, whipped cream.
Opposite: Bird Series No. 8, Qian Gang, oil on canvas, 2012.

CHARITY

There is so much
natural *beauty*
all around us,
and it's *transient,*
like butterflies.
I created the
PINK REVOLUTION
cake to support
Hong Kong Cancer Fund.

Pink Revolution: Crème fraîche butter cake, strawberry jam, sugar hearts, sugar butterflies.

Venus: White chocolate and blueberry marble cake, sugar ruffles, sugar pearls, sugar peonies.

flowers. pearls. ruffles.

LOVE AT FIRST BITE

When you send fresh flowers as a gift, you can't be sure what state they'll be in when they're delivered.

But a sugar flower is always perfect. Especially when it's packaged with a love letter.

Above: Sugar peony. Right: Fresh flowers.

It was the day I opened C'est La B in Tai Hang.
We were burning incense and I was saying my prayers to the sky when suddenly
a butterfly landed on my shoulder and perched for a while.
Hong Kong is very built-up, choked with traffic,
and seeing butterflies among the skyscrapers is rare.

satin
silk
lace
chiffon
organza
cashmere
velvet
angora
feathers
chinchilla
linen
peachskin

BUTTERFLY KISSES IS PURE AND WHITE ON THE OUTSIDE, BUT THEN YOU CUT IT OPEN – OH! THE COLORS! I'VE ALWAYS LIKED SURPRISES.

Butterfly Kisses: Rainbow chiffon, whipped cream, pear compote, red berries, peach, kiwifruit, hand-painted sugar butterflies.

The play of light creates magic, whether it's reflected off sequins or the sea. And I love the view from the terrace at SEVVA by night, when the steel exoskeleton of Lord Norman Foster's HSBC building is lit from within.

Halloween was my inspiration for Death by Chocolate. The skull hides a secret opening for a letter.
Death by Chocolate: Champagne chocolate truffle cake, berry sauce, Swarovski diamante skull.

Hong Kong is a city of contrasts – rich and poor, high-rise and low-rise – but surprising synchronicities too. This is the Bank of China Tower by I.M. Pei, whose design was inspired by the growth patterns of bamboo.

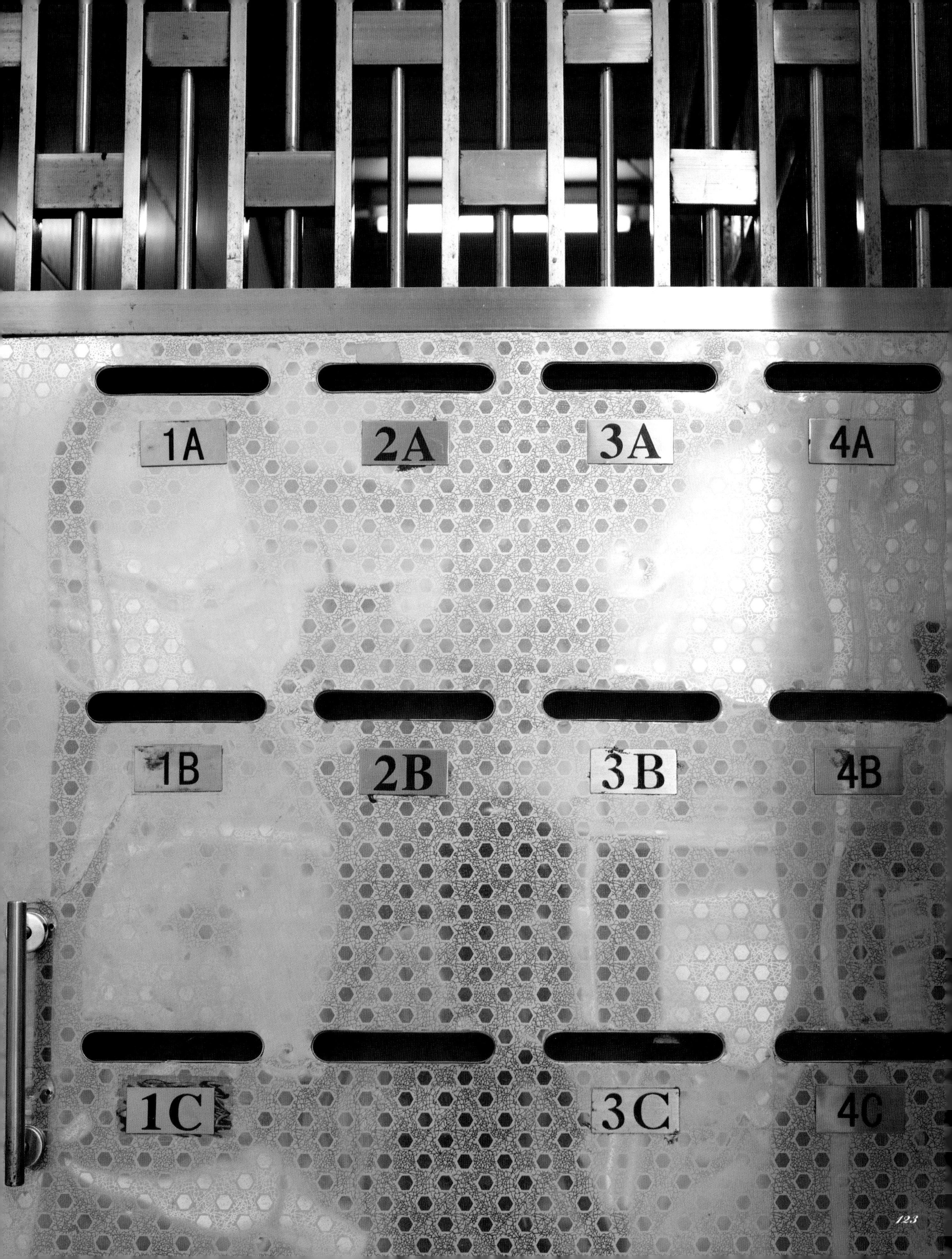
1A
2A
3A
4A
1B
2B
3B
4B
1C
3C
4C

Although I'm in hospitality and design, fashion will always be in my blood.
Here's to the monochrome craze of spring/summer 2013.
Monochrome Glamour: Dark chocolate mousse, white chocolate mousse, chocolate crisps, chocolate ganache.

MONO
CHRO
MATIC
MOD.

A hot, sweet soup of black sesame, cane sugar and a few grains of rice, blended to a creamy texture, is a Chinese favorite.
I found the bowl, which is part of a set, in Kyoto. It's very fine, almost translucent.

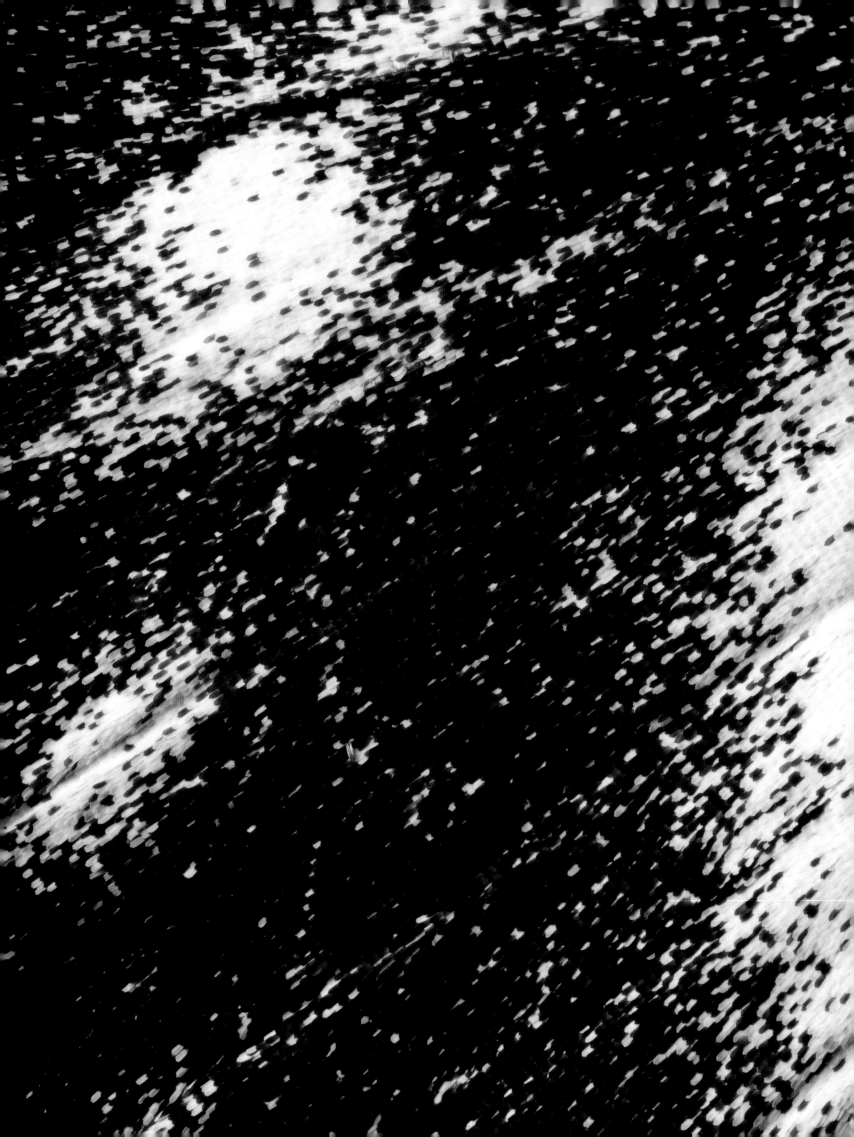

'His talent was as natural as the
pattern that was made by the dust on a butterfly's wings.'
ERNEST HEMINGWAY ON F. SCOTT FITZGERALD,
A Moveable Feast

At the flower market, chrysanthemum buds are individually wrapped, protected as tenderly as babies.

Maidenhair ferns grow on the 15-metre *garden* wall at SEVVA. This cake is *dedicated* to their *delicacy* and frailty.

Garden Beauty: Chocolate caramel chiffon, sugar agave, sugar fern.

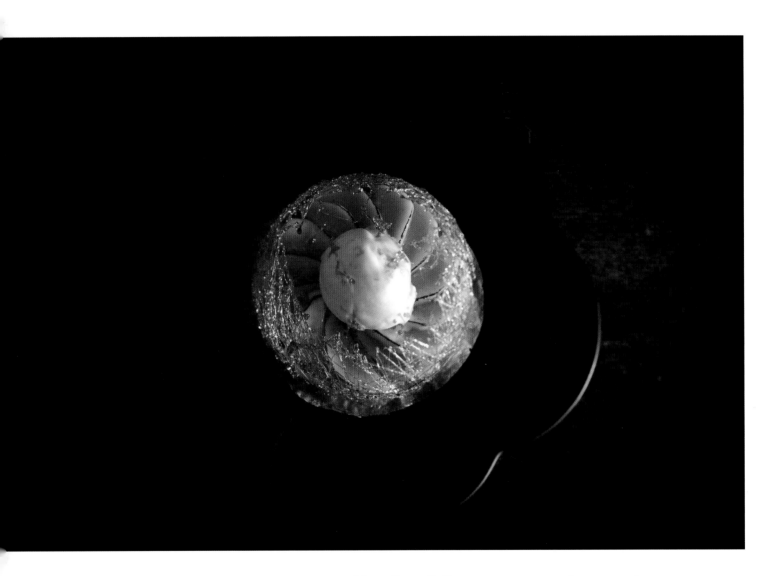

Mango Tango: Puff pastry, mango, mango glaze, mango ice-cream, spun sugar.

Treasures from my personal collection of homewares: The teapot is such a gem, handmade from sterling silver, jade and gold. The 24-carat gold-leaf teacup and saucer are from Limoges in France.

PROSPERITY
RICHES
POWER
ABUNDANCE
ALCHEMY
AURUM
WORTH
WEALTH
AFFLUENCE
LUXURY
OPULENCE
TREASURE
PRECIOUSNESS
SUNLIGHT
SHIMMER
SPARKLE
LUSTRE
SHINE
GLOW
GLISTER
GILT
GIFTS
JEWELLERY
BRACELET
CHARM
LOCKET
NECKLACE
BROOCH
REWARD
AWARD
REGALIA
DECORATION
DISTINCTION
HONOR
ACCOLADE
ORNAMENT
GOLDFINCH
GOLDFISH

D

My friend Gladys Perint Palmer is one of the best fashion illustrators in the world today.
This is one of the sketches she drew for me for Sevva.

My mother loved mah-jong, and I grew up listening to its familiar shuffling sounds.

When we were styling this photo, I was reminded of the beautiful mah-jong sets my father gave to Eleanor.

I was thinking of the Paul McCartney–Stevie Wonder song when I named this cake.
Music is a universal language, a beautiful language.
Ebony & Ivory: Black sesame and coconut butter cake, shredded coconut.

TRANSFORMATION

A cake kitchen is very different from a restaurant kitchen, where the woks are flying and it's boiling hot.

My pastry chefs all love what they do: they create. They say cooking gives people joy, and they put a lot of energy into it.

And that energy transforms them. I like that energy. It's a good energy. Nothing harsh or angry. The cakery is very heartfelt for me.

You just need to touch someone, just a little touch, in their heart, and you've helped a lot. It transforms people.

OUR CHOCOLATE
is a combination
of *five of the best*
chocolates
in the world.
It's a *secret*
my friend *shared*
with me when
he was *right*
hand to *Madame*
Lenôtre of the
famous
Paris pâtisserie.

LOVE FEELS LIKE BUTTERFLIES INSIDE.

154

Better than Sex: Chocolate fudge cake, crushed toffee, caramel crunch, chocolate wafer crisps, salted toffee sauce, sugar lips.

CAKE
RAPTURE
THERE ARE
A *LOT OF LAYERS*
IN BETTER THAN SEX.
WE PUT ***CRUSHED***
TOFFEE AND WAFER
CRISPS INSIDE SO THAT
WHEN YOU ***BITE***
INTO IT – CRUNCH.
AND WE POUR
TOFFEE SAUCE
OVER THE TOP.
WHAT DOES THE TOFFEE
SAUCE REPRESENT?
WHAT DO YOU
WANT IT
TO REPRESENT?

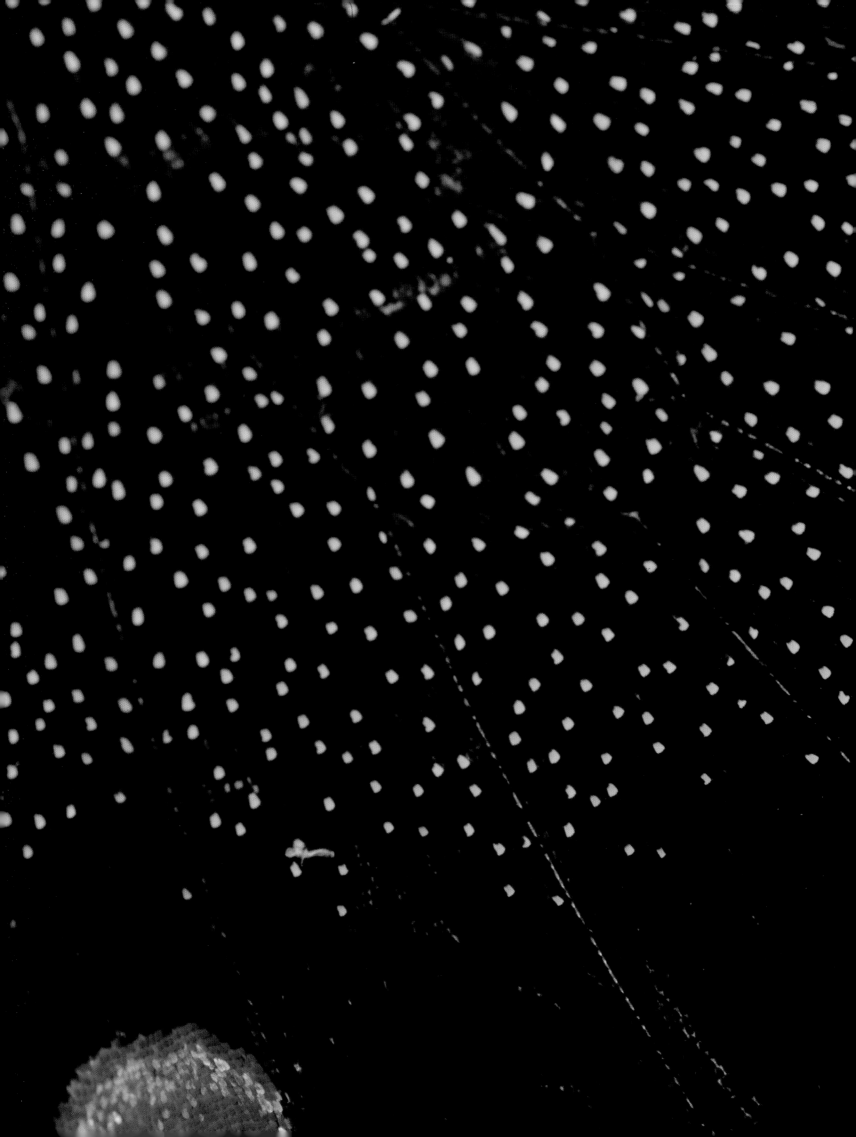

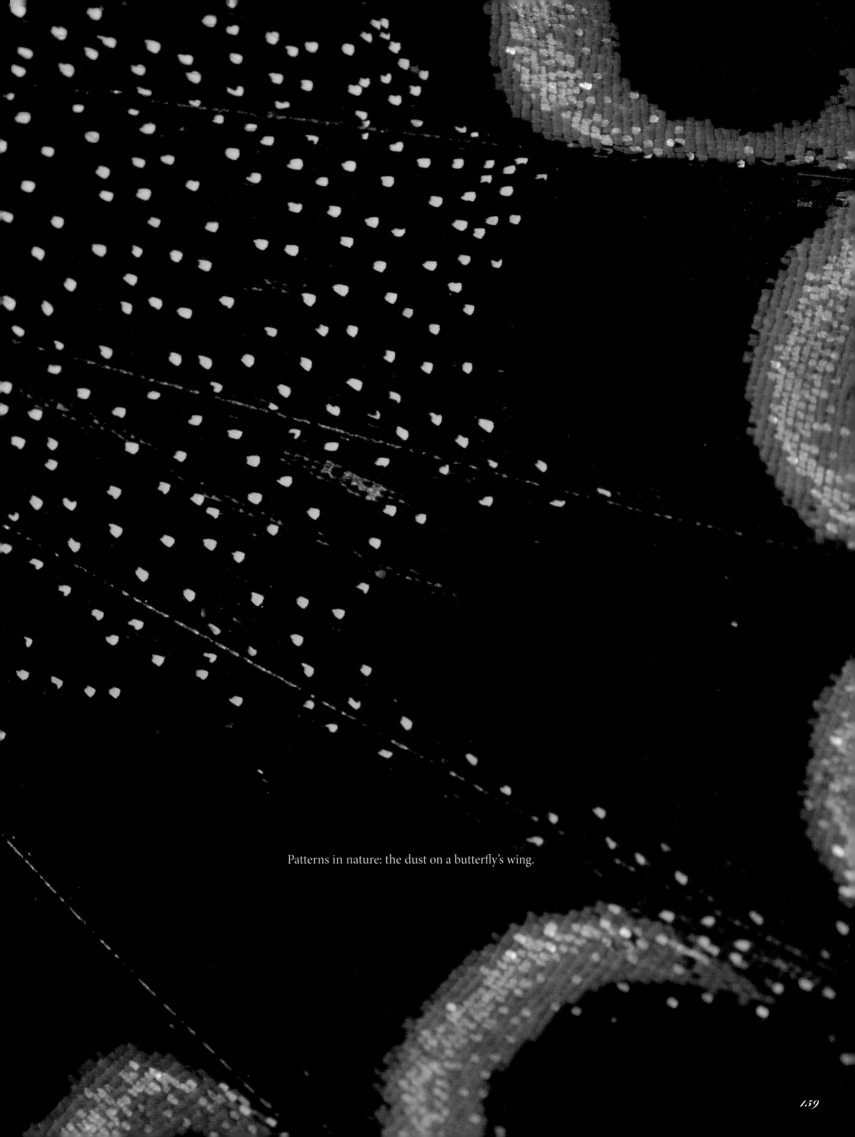

Patterns in nature: the dust on a butterfly's wing.

My favorite ribbon stores are in Sham Shui Po.
This rich red piece tones in with the sugar camellia, and when I saw it,
I thought of Scarlett O'Hara.
Scarlet: Marbled vanilla and red berry Victoria sponge, sugar camellias.

RED

HEAT
FIRE
EXPLOSION
FLAMES
CREATIVITY
ENERGY
INTENSITY
MOTIVATION
POWER
DRAMA
COURAGE
STRENGTH
WARMTH
LOVE
ROSES
BLUSH
VELVET
ROUGE
ROSSO
ROJO
RÖD
RAUTT
HENNA
COCHINEAL
BERRIES
CHERRIES
RUBIES
GARNETS
NEGRONI
POMEGRANATES
GRENACHE
CHILLIES
LOBSTER
SUMMER
REBELLION
SEDUCTION
TANGO
SCARLET
PASSION
AROUSAL
FEVER
BLOOD
VIRILITY
SENSUALITY
EXCITEMENT
ENERGY
FEROCITY
SPEED
HEART
GLOW
LIPS
NIPPLES
FIREWORKS
EMBERS

In Chinese culture, the color red traditionally symbolizes joy and good fortune.
Double Happiness: Crème fraîche butter cake, red beans.

Take my picture

Be Gaga'd: Chocolate chiffon, grape jelly, blueberries, Oreos, chocolate spikes, silver sugar pearls, marshmallows.

Hollywood! <small>LADY GAGA</small>

'I search for the realness, the real feeling of a subject,
all the texture around it... I always want to see the third dimension of something...
I want to come alive with the object.'
ANDREW WYETH

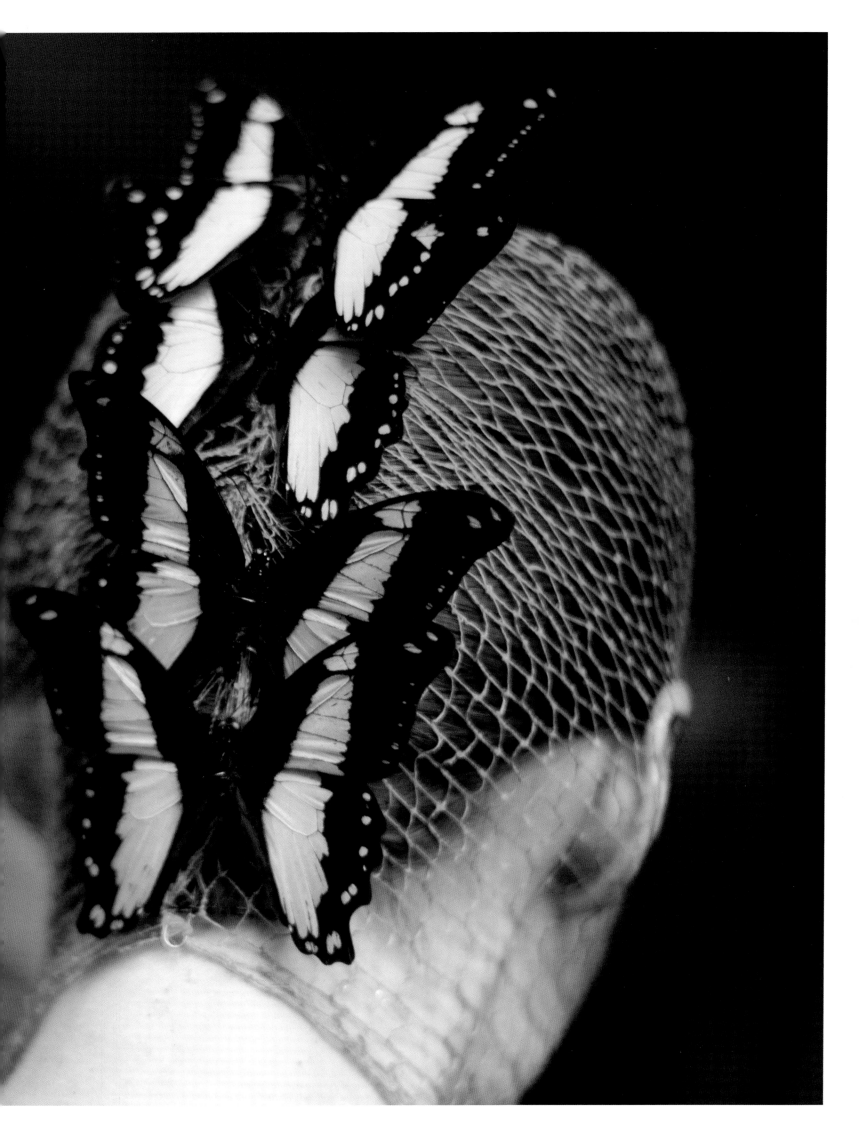

*Madame Butterfly: Beetroot, pistachio and chocolate chiffon, apricot compote,
whipped cream, hand-painted sugar butterfly.*

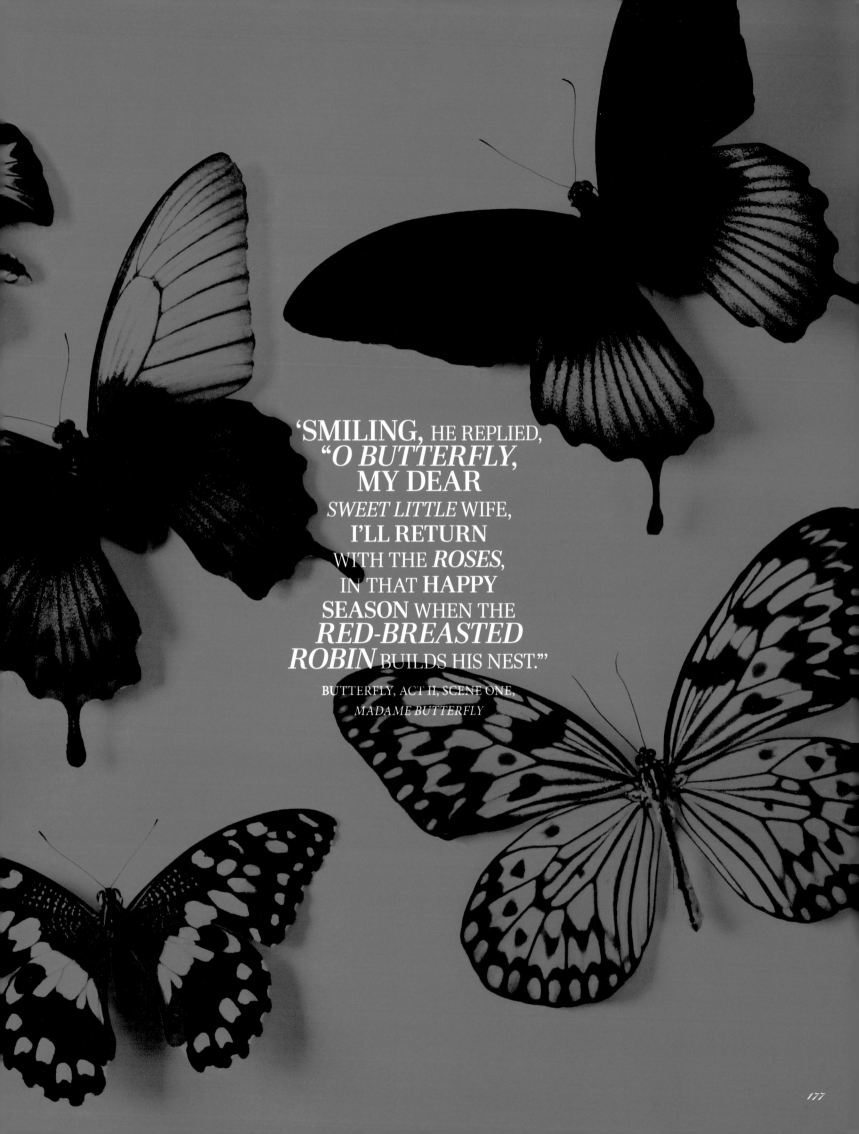

'SMILING, HE REPLIED,
"O BUTTERFLY,
MY DEAR
SWEET LITTLE WIFE,
I'LL RETURN
WITH THE *ROSES*,
IN THAT HAPPY
SEASON WHEN THE
*RED-BREASTED
ROBIN* BUILDS HIS NEST."

BUTTERFLY, ACT II, SCENE ONE,
MADAME BUTTERFLY

When I saw a dress adorned with pansies in Dior's spring/summer 2013
haute couture collection, I was inspired. Thank you, Raf!
Pansy Couture: Chocolate cake, passionfruit mousse, chocolate ganache, sugar pansies.

C'est La B café-bar

The graphic look of our cake boxes inspired my design for the black-and-white-striped marble floor at C'est La B.
When you enter the café, no matter what sort of day you've had, you feel enveloped, cocooned,
in a space that's a complete departure from the outside world.

STORYTIME
My sister, Joyce Ma, has a home in Palais Royale. I'll always remember the first time
she took me for tea in the gardens and told me stories of Marie Antoinette, who used to live there.
Marie Antoinette's Crave: Pistachio chiffon, rose-petal jam, whipped cream,
raspberries, rainbow macarons, dragées, cotton candy.

a cake fit for a queen.

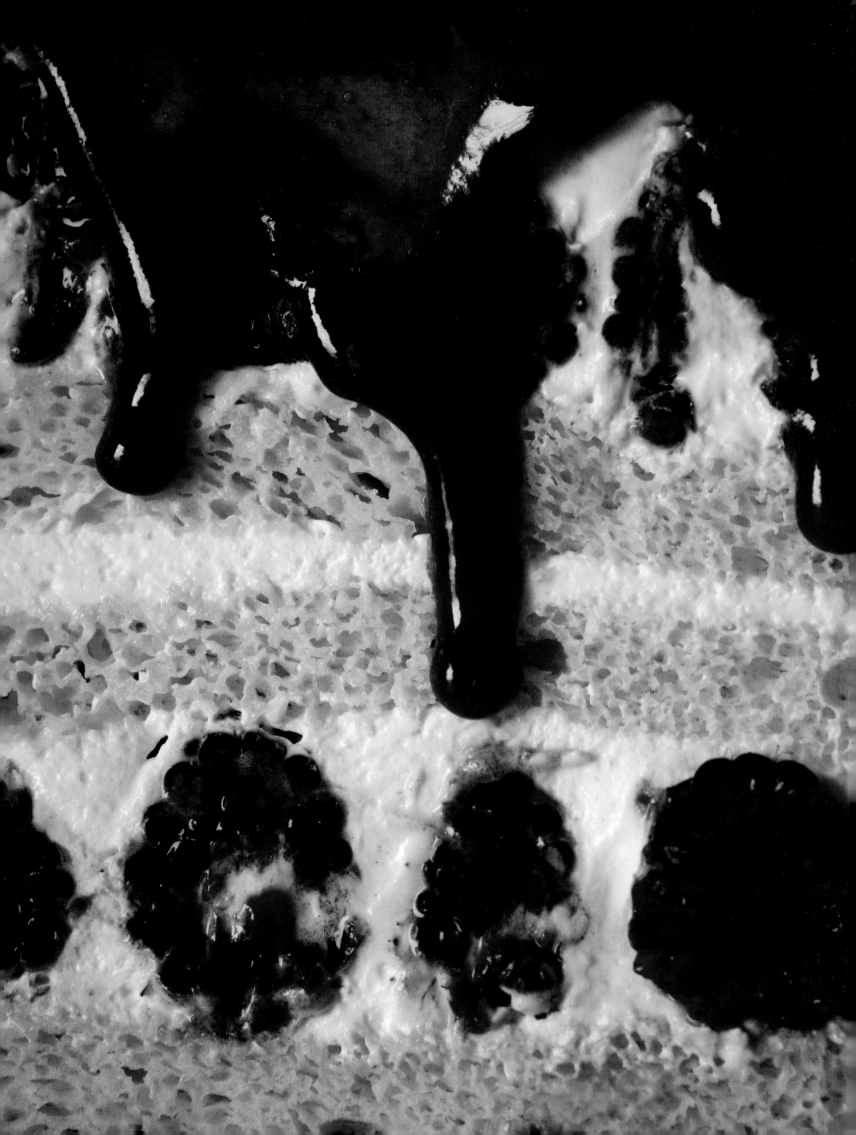

Ms B's Cakery opened on the same day Prince William and Kate Middleton were married, April 29, 2011, and I thought, Marie Antoinette is lonely – I've got to find her a prince. So I drummed up Le Louis. Fantasies blow me away. *Le Louis: Chocolate chiffon, blackberries, blueberries, whipped cream, marshmallows, dragées, cotton candy (below, right).*

'Le compliment,
c'est quelque
chose comme
le baiser
à travers le voile.
La volupté
y met sa
douce pointe,
tout en se cachant.'

A compliment is something like a kiss through a veil.
Voluptuousness mingles there
with its sweet tiny point, while it hides itself.
VICTOR HUGO, *Les Misérables*

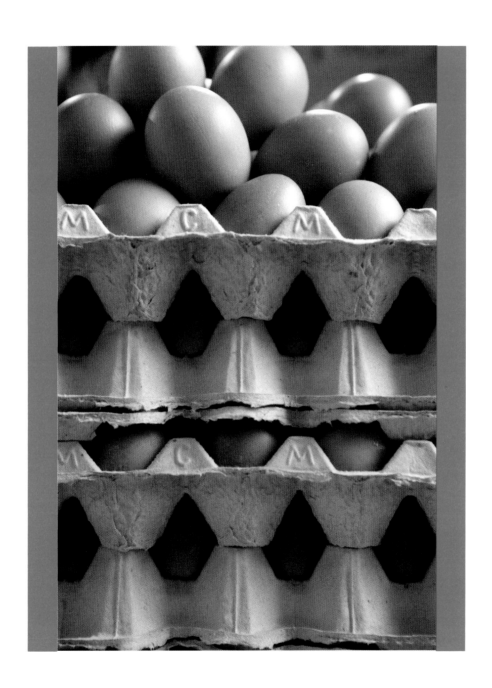

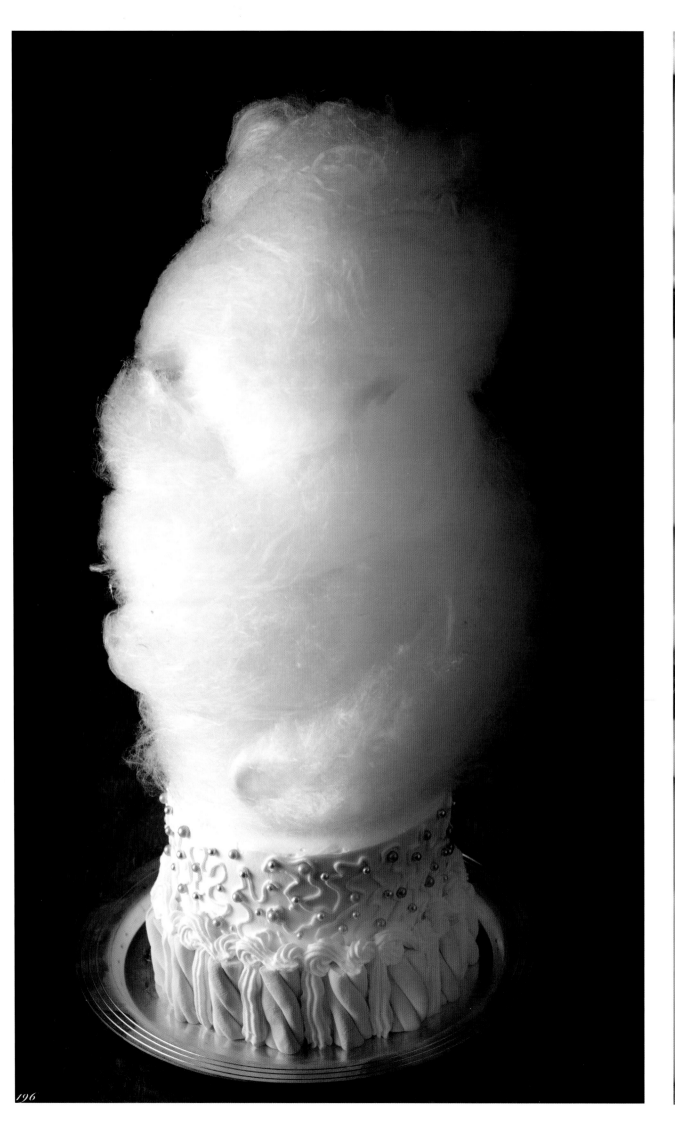

巴黎

Paris used to be my second home.

Chester: French vanilla chiffon, chestnut purée, meringue, whipped cream, Champagne macarons.

chester.

'[The butterfly] flew against the window pane, and was seen
and admired by those in the room, who caught him,
and stuck him on a pin, in a box of curiosities. They could not do more for him.

"Now I am perched on a stalk, like the flowers," said the butterfly.
"It is not very pleasant, certainly; I should imagine it is something like being married;
for here I am stuck fast." And with this thought he consoled himself a little.'
HANS CHRISTIAN ANDERSEN, *The Butterfly*

Baking requires precision and patience. Peeling the chestnuts,
beating the meringue, whisking the cream – you need to be patient and gentle.

This work by Sir Peter Blake shows the flower market that is such an inspiration for me. *Flower Street, Hong Kong, Sir Peter Blake, silkscreen print, edition of 88.*

Hongkong

sunshine.

Sunshine: Lemon and poppyseed chiffon, lemon curd, whipped cream, crushed meringue, sugar poppies.

'There are painters who transform the sun into a yellow spot, but there are others who, with the help of their art and their intelligence, transform a yellow spot into the sun.'

Pablo Picasso

PURITY

We use *fresh* ingredients such as *purple taro* and *beetroot* to create the colors for some of my cakes. All that chopping and boiling to get *vibrant* yet *natural* shades is an enormous amount of work but worth the effort. *It's what's on the inside that counts.*

Paradise: Taro chiffon, ube cream, macapuno coconut.
Opposite: Bird Series No. 1, Qian Gang, oil on canvas, 2012.

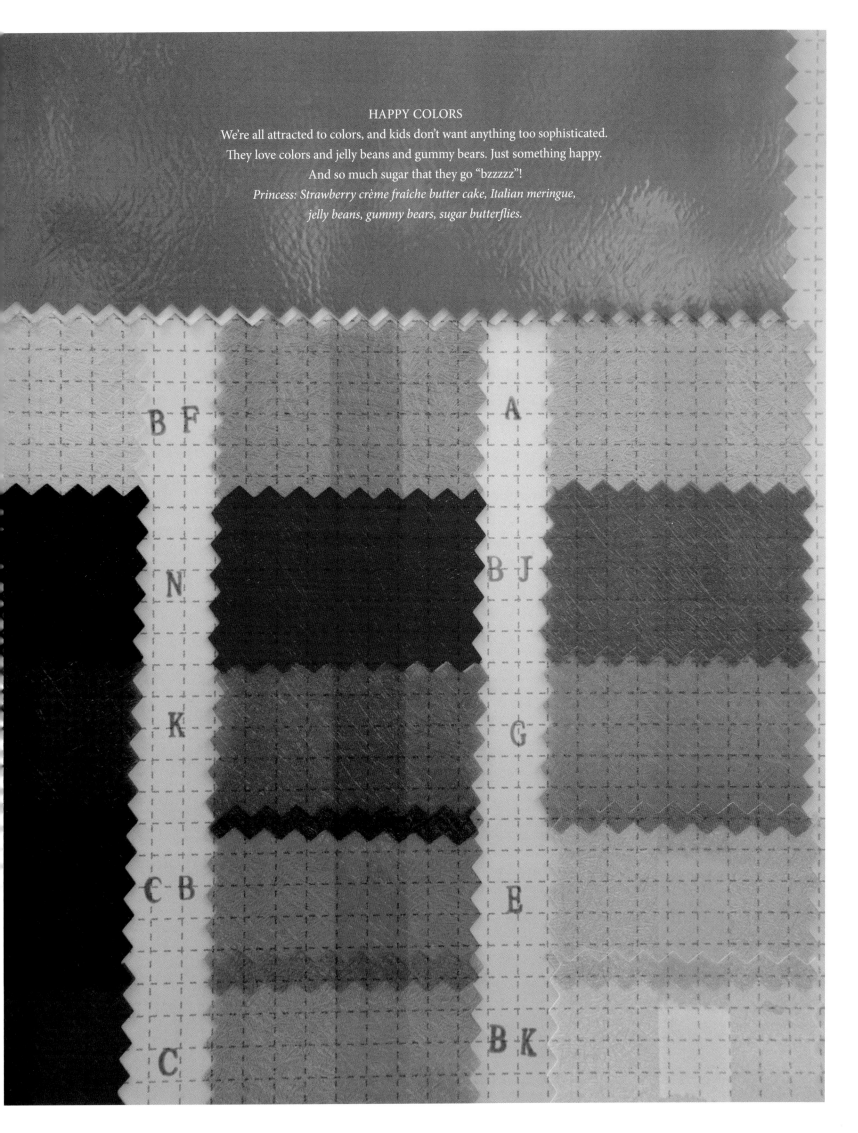

HAPPY COLORS

We're all attracted to colors, and kids don't want anything too sophisticated.
They love colors and jelly beans and gummy bears. Just something happy.
And so much sugar that they go "bzzzzz"!
Princess: Strawberry crème fraîche butter cake, Italian meringue,
jelly beans, gummy bears, sugar butterflies.

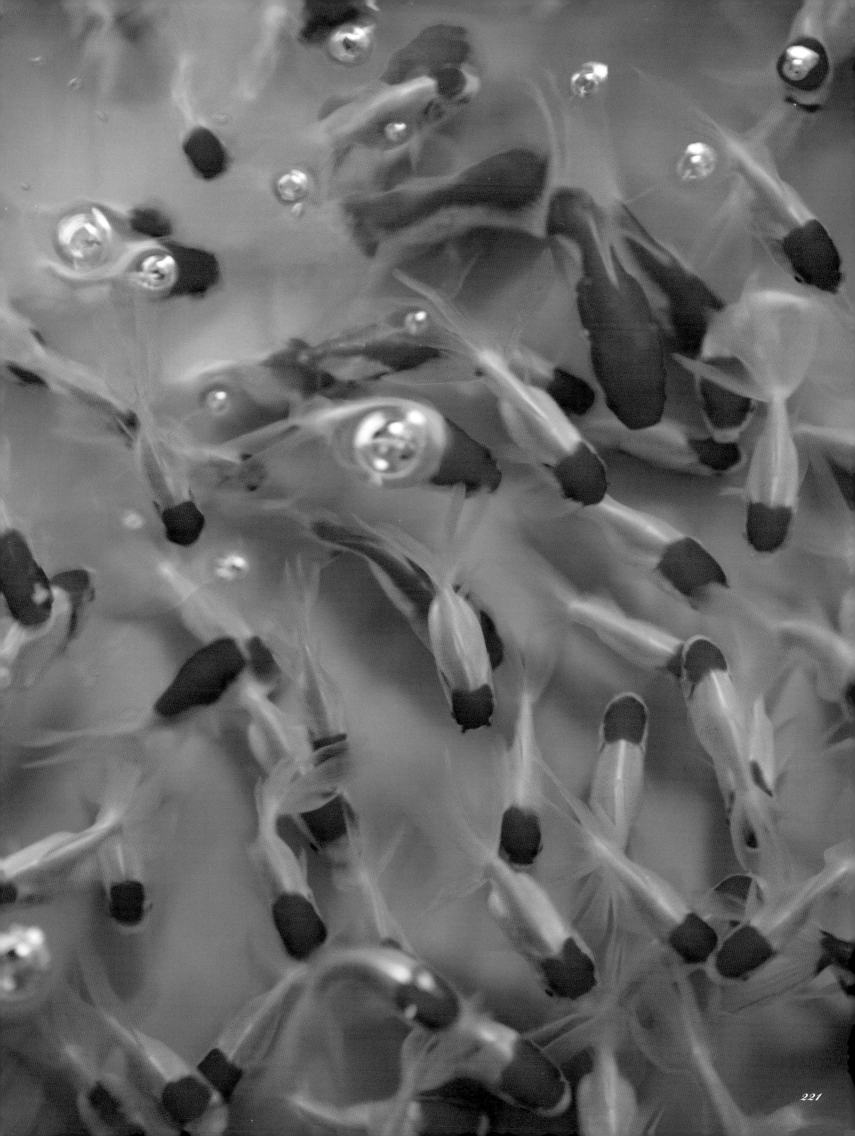

221

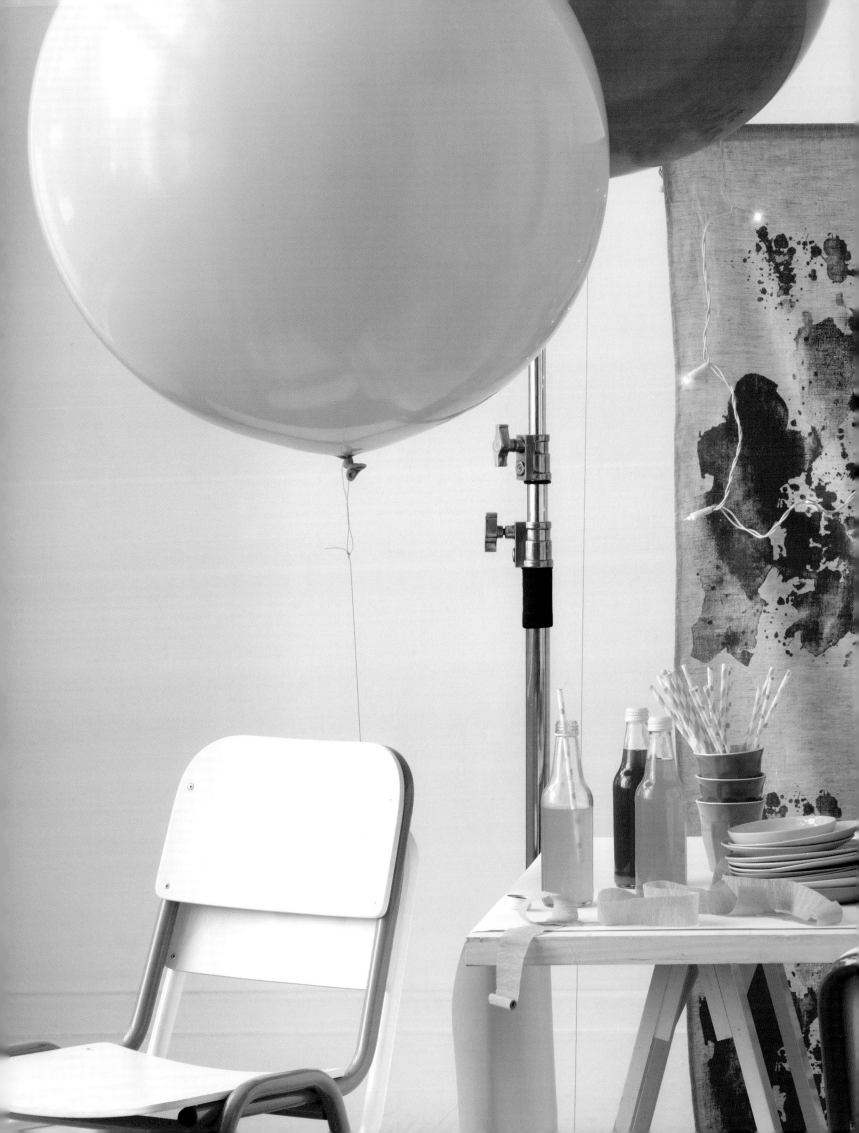

party.

INNOCENCE AND EXPERIENCE
When I turned six, I had a huge Humpty Dumpty
birthday cake. Humpty Dumpty sat on a wall surrounded by
intricately made soldiers. I loved it, and when I'm designing cakes
for children, I think like a child. I'm always with young people,
and I have a childlike mind. I'm inspired by memories
of my own childhood – candy apples, music boxes,
multicolored licorice, carousels, cotton candy, balloons.
I know how it was, I know how it should be, and I interpret it.
All creative people are like that.

Whoopie: Red velvet beetroot cake, cream cheese frosting, handmade licorice allsorts (opposite, top row, centre).
The Little Prince: Chocolate cake, Maltesers, French vanilla crème anglaise, melted gummy bears (opposite, bottom row, left).
Smartie Pants: Chocolate truffle cake, toffee-covered nuts, oversize Smarties (below).

Send in the Clowns: Raspberry and chocolate butter cake, old-fashioned candies, sugar balloons.

Pansy: Vanilla chiffon, pineapple bavarois, fresh pineapple, sugar pansies (opposite).

Sir Peter Blake's work shows Queens Road in Hong Kong, where I have my office. *Hong Kong, Queens Road, Central*, Sir Peter Blake, silkscreen print, edition of 88.

I'M
PASSIONATE.
WITHOUT
PASSION
YOU
CAN'T
DO
ANYTHING.

Chiffon, rose jam, raspberries (background). Sunshine, taster size (cake stand, upper level).
Pâte à choux, lychee cream or mango cream (cake stand, lower level).

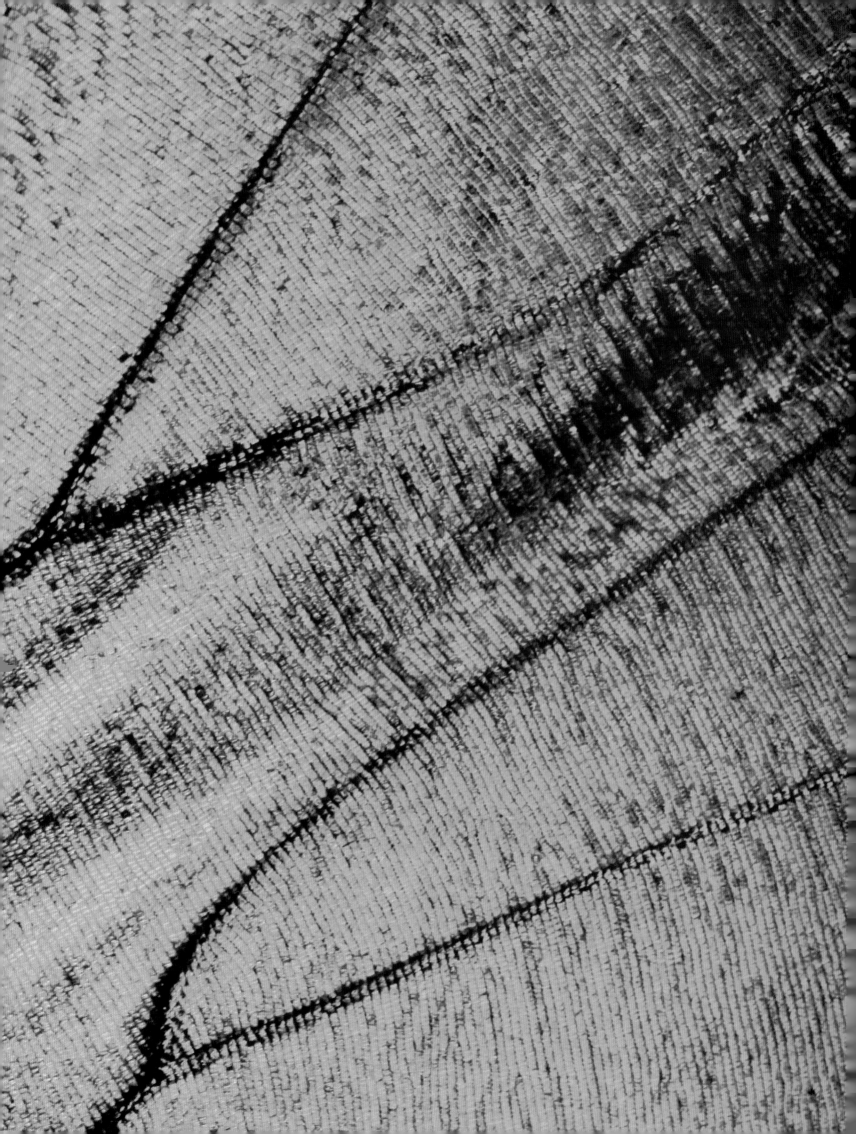

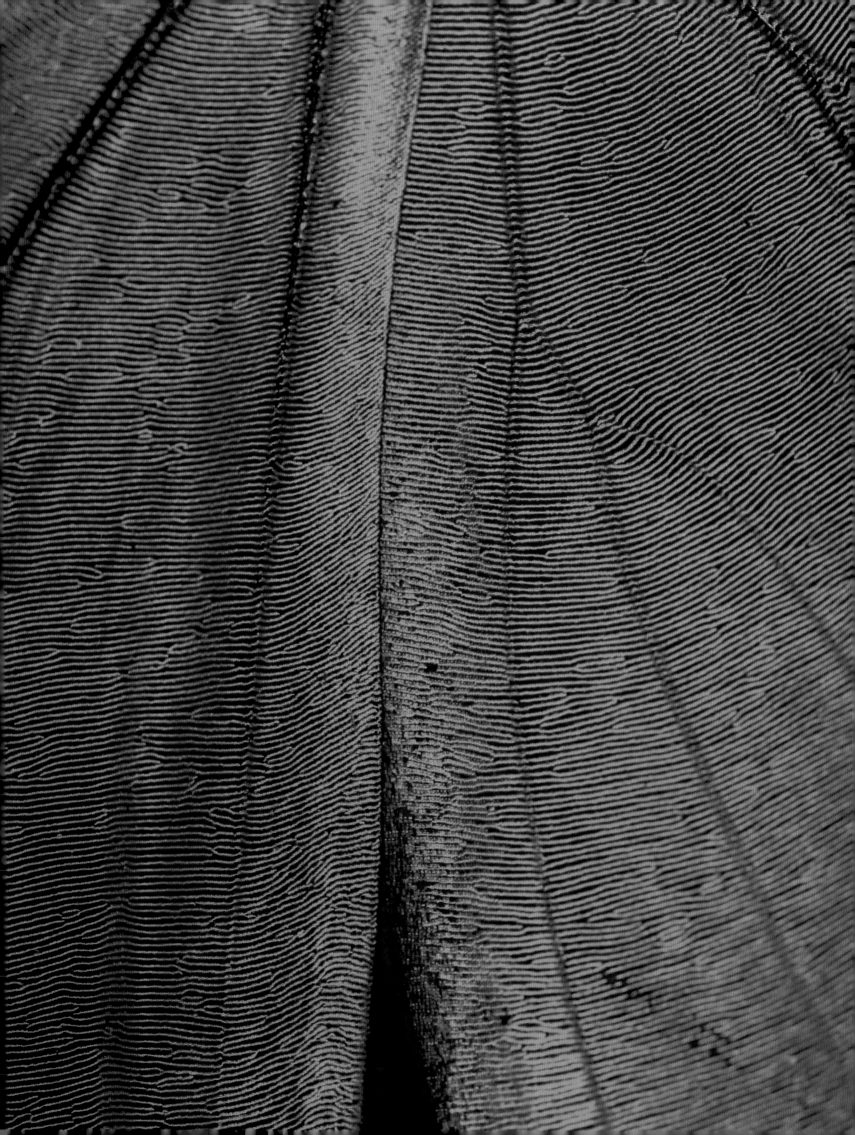

THE UNFURLING OF HAPPINESS

Nothing gives me more pleasure than *giving joy to people*. People write to me to say *thank you*. *Seriously*, they get really *excited* over *a piece of cake*.

#21   #

#23   #26

#33   #34

#35   #37

245

'The butterfly counts
not months but moments,
and has time enough.'
RABINDRANATH TAGORE

WHERE
DOES YOUR CREATIVITY
COME FROM?

My inspiration
comes from the
accumulated knowledge
and experience of
my blessedly privileged
background and
from years of working
in creative industries,
particularly fashion.

It also comes from
having a great mentor:
I owe so much to my
sister, Joyce Ma,
who was the doyenne of
fashion in the East.
As her right hand for
many years, I worked
on hundreds of creative
projects. And throughout
my life she's exposed me
to fashion, travel, and
a lifestyle which is
simply the ultimate.
Later I became
the Regional Chief
of Image &
Communications
for Chanel Asia Pacific.
This position gave me
lots more opportunities
to conceptualize and
produce unforgettable
events across Asia.>

< One of the most
memorable shows
I created for Chanel
involved taking
over a Shanghai airfield
that hadn't been
open in 30 years.
We had 150 uniformed
men lining the road
for miles, saluting from
their guard posts as the
guests drove in.
We created landing lights
on the airfield,
just like an operating
airport, and we towed
in a plane painted
with the Chanel logo.
Laser beams flashed
across the sky, and the
glow of hundreds of huge
candle-lanterns scattered
in the fields illuminated
the one-mile perimeter.
But that's just one event
of many, too many to
name, and Chanel is only
one influence among
many in my life.

So you see, my creativity
doesn't come from
online or from
magazines, but from
total immersion:
international jetsetting
from a young age;
rich exposure to
the great cities, the
great restaurants, of
the world and beyond –
Paris, Tokyo, Milan,
London, New York.

FASHION AND BAKING:
WHAT DO THEY
HAVE IN COMMON?

In fashion, if you've
got great pieces to start
with, you can mix
and match and always
look fabulous.
The components of my
cakes are like that.
I choose to work
with pretty things,
beautiful things.
I want to uplift people,
even a little bit.
I'm always taking pictures
of whatever inspires me.
It could be a splash
of color, a page from a
book, flowers, an artwork.
What could be more
beautiful? But my
cakes are a matter of
balance, of going beyond
appearances. Some
other cakes are all about
the moulded sugar art.
They're very
one-dimensional, and
there's nothing to taste.
My cakes have bite;
they have layers
of different textures
and flavours.
You can taste the quality.
They're delicious
to eat as well
as beautifully crafted.

YOU'VE OFTEN SAID
YOUR CAKES
HAVE INTEGRITY.
WHAT DO YOU MEAN?

Look at the way
we prepare the mango
jam for our cake
Moonstruck'd.
It's made in fine
home kitchens in
the Philippines
during mango season,
using only prime
tree-ripened mangoes.
They're cooked when
they're very ripe
and very sweet, so they
need hardly any sugar,
and stirred slowly
on a very low heat for
more than five hours.
It smells so good!
And it's the very
essence of mango.
The taste of our cakes
is so important.

THE CONVERSATION HOUR
COFFE AND CAKE WITH **BONNAE GOKSON**

YOUR THREE VENTURES – SEVVA, MS B'S CAKERY AND C'EST LA B – ARE ALL VERY DIFFERENT, BUT LINKED BY YOUR CAKES. TELL US ABOUT THE JOURNEY.

SEVVA was born after much contemplation following a sabatical. It also involved a lot of persuasion from good friends who wanted me to re-create what I'd done for Joyce Cafes. When I was growing up, parties were grand, stylish affairs, so to some extent, it was a natural progression. I'd been trained in the arts of hospitality and entertaining from a very young age. SEVVA is like a home to me, and I love dressing up a home and applying my creativity to it. And of course I love food!

At SEVVA, drinks are served in one area, dinner in another, then you adjourn to the terrace or to the Taste Bar. 'SEVVA' in Sanskrit, spelled s-e-v-a, means selfless service, or 'I bow to the honor of service.' But SEVVA's pastry kitchen is tiny, and our cakes were much in demand, so I decided to open a central kitchen to help out >

< with the many orders and events coming in. Then I thought why don't I find a space in a less expensive area of town and have a commissary as well as a little area to sell from, and that was the start of Ms B's Cakery. That neighborhood, NoHo, is now one of the hippest areas in town, and it all began with Ms B's.

The next stage in the journey was the opening of C'est La B, where you can sit down and have a good cup of tea and a casual meal. I wanted to create a particular atmosphere. Many designers are doing neutral, pastel, pretty-pretty interiors. But I wanted something different for C'est La B, something quite gutsy, bold, with a lot of character. When you have dark décor, your cakes pop out. They are the stars peeping out from the dark skies.

WHAT'S THE STORY BEHIND THE ARTWORKS IN YOUR BOOK?

On a recent trip to Shanghai, I spotted Chinese artist Qian Gang's works of nature and instantly fell in love with his paintings. Being Chinese myself, I felt that showing his art in my book was the right thing to do. (See pages 42–43, page 99 and page 216.) His amazing sense of color sparked my imagination and provided further inspiration for my cakes.

Sir Peter Blake is Britain's answer to Andy Warhol. He's perhaps most famous for having created the cover artwork for the Beatles album *Sgt. Pepper's Lonely Hearts Club Band*. I'm very fortunate to own his butterflies series. (See pages 206–207 and 236–237).

My friend Gladys Perint Palmer is one of the best fashion illustrators in the world today, and I've also included two of the sketches she drew for me for SEVVA. (See page 145 and page 232.)

And the detail in the butterflies' wings is amazing. When we selected the macro photographs for this book, we made several research trips to the Australian Museum in Sydney, which has one of the larger collections of Australian specimens in the world. I'll never tire of looking at butterflies in all their variety.

Being able to surround myself with such beautiful images is a blessing.

HOW DO YOU RELAX?

Away from my businesses, I have a very simple life. I live up in the hills facing a reservoir surrounded by the most beautiful nature trails. It's a place where I can take time out to reflect and go for hikes. I'm like a very old soul. I spend time with my friends too – we might go for brunch, a facial and a massage, and of course we talk the whole time. And I have a huge library of music for every mood.

Look, I don't even bake. What I do with my cakes is translate. My greatest satisfaction comes from giving people joy. It's just a piece of cake, but I believe that if you can give people a split-second thrill of happiness when they receive and taste your cake, why not? People write to tell me how happy their parents-in-law or their friends or their colleagues were with their cake. It's such an uplifting pleasure to give.

LET THEM EAT CAKE

I THANK

MY FAMILY, THE TWO WOMEN IN PARTICULAR.
FIRST, MY MOTHER, **ELEANOR**, WHO WAS A STUNNING BEAUTY
WITH MANY TALENTS. I MAY NOT HAVE INHERITED HER LOOKS
BUT I AM THANKFUL TO HAVE INHERITED HER FLAIR AND TALENTS.
AND MY SISTER **JOYCE**, MY 'AUNTIE MAME',
WHO HAS GIVEN ME SO MUCH ENCOURAGEMENT AND EXPOSED ME
TO THE WORLD I KNOW TODAY.

MY FRIEND **GINNY ROCES DE GUZMAN**, WHO HELPED ME WITH
THE RECIPE FOR THE CAKE THAT STARTED IT ALL, THE ORIGINAL CARAMEL
CRUNCH CAKE. FROM THIS I DREAMED AND CREATED MORE.

MY CAKERY TEAM. I'VE WORKED SO CLOSELY WITH THEM
AND I THANK THEM FOR ACCEPTING MY CRAZY IDEAS AND TURNING
THEM INTO REALITY. I'M ESPECIALLY GRATEFUL FOR THE DEDICATION AND
LOYALTY OF CHEF **DANIEL KOON**, WHO STARTED WITH ME AT JOYCE
CAFE UMPTEEN YEARS AGO AND STILL REMAINS A STEADY ANCHOR.

JOHN LEE, WHO HAS WEATHERED LONG HOURS IN FRONT
OF A MONITOR WORKING ON IMAGES UNTIL THEY WERE PERFECT.
I'M SO GRATEFUL FOR YOUR DEDICATION AND KINDNESS.

A. CHESTER ONG, FOR YOUR GREAT TEAMWORK AND PATIENCE
ON COUNTLESS SUNDAYS OF PHOTO SHOOTS.

MY AUSSIE SUPERGIRLS:
KATE DENNIS (*CREATIVE DIRECTOR*), **PETRINA TINSLAY** (*PHOTOGRAPHER*),
EMMA KNOWLES (*STYLIST*) AND **KERRYN BURGESS** (*WRITER*).

MY BELOVED OFFICE TEAM FOR THEIR SUPPORT AND
HARD WORK IN COUNTLESS WAYS.

THE MANY FANS AND CUSTOMERS WHO HAVE
SUPPORTED MY WORK OVER THE YEARS.

HONG KONG, *MY HOME CITY, THE PLACE OF MY ROOTS
AND THE SOURCE OF MUCH OF MY CREATIVE INSPIRATION.* I'M GRATEFUL TO
HAVE HAD THE OPPORTUNITY TO CONTRIBUTE TO THE CITY
AND TO REPRESENT IT BEFORE AN INTERNATIONAL READERSHIP.

I'VE CHOSEN TO CREATE A BUSINESS THAT EXUDES LIFE,
HAPPINESS, GOOD HUMOR AND GOOD ENERGY; THAT BRINGS
MOMENTS OF SWEETNESS INTO EVERY DAY.
I PRACTICE GRATITUDE EVERY DAY FOR MY MANY BLESSINGS.

BONNAE GOKSON

SEVVA
www.sevva.hk

Prince's Building 25/F
10 Chater Road
Central
Hong Kong
(852) 2537 1388

MS B's CAKERY
www.msbscakery.hk

39 Gough Street
Central
Hong Kong
(852) 2815 8303

C'EST LA B
www.msbscakery.hk/cestlab.html

Shop 202
Level 2, Pacific Place
Admiralty
Hong Kong
(852) 2536 0173

Shop 3
G/F 110–114 Tung Lo Wan Road
Tai Hang
Hong Kong
(852) 2806 8168

Shop G111
G/F Gateway Arcade,
Harbour City
Tsim Sha Tsui
Hong Kong
(852) 3102 2838

PUBLISHED BY
GOFF BOOKS
AN IMPRINT OF
ORO EDITIONS

Gordon Goff:
Publisher
www.oroeditions.com
info@oroeditions.com

Copyright © 2013
ORO Editions
ISBN 978 1 939621 01 6
1st edition
10 9 8 7 6 5 4 3 2 1

Design by
Kate Dennis,
This Is Ikon
www.thisisikon.com

Photography by
Petrina Tinslay
and
A. Chester Ong

Edited by
Kerryn Burgess

Supplementary
photography by
Benoît Peverelli
(pages 20–21)
Kevin Tachman
(pages 30–31, 72–73,
108–109, 130–131,
cover and 150–151,
172–173, 246–247)
Renaud Visage / Getty Images
(pages 36–37)
Katrin Backes
(pages 182–183)
Peter Frank / Corbis
(licorice allsorts page 226)
Ocean / Corbis
(round candies page 227)

*Hong Kong,
Queen's Road, Central*
Silkscreen print
98cm x 70cm
Edition of 88
Published by CCA Galleries
Printed at
Coriander Studio, London
© Peter Blake.
All rights reserved,
DACS 2013

Flower Street, Hong Kong
Silkscreen Print
98cm x 70cm
Edition of 88
Published by CCA Galleries
Printed at
Coriander Studio, London
© Peter Blake.
All rights reserved,
DACS 2013

Bird Series No. 1
Oil on canvas, 2012
© Qian Gang and
Elisabeth de Brabant Chinese
Contemporary Fine Art

Bird Series No. 6
Oil on canvas, 2012
© Qian Gang and
Elisabeth de Brabant Chinese
Contemporary Fine Art

Bird Series No. 8
Oil on canvas, 2012
© Qian Gang and
Elisabeth de Brabant Chinese
Contemporary Fine Art

SEVVA artworks
(page 145
and page 232) by
Gladys Perint Palmer
www.gladysperintpalmer.com

Color separations
and printing:
ORO Group Ltd
Printed in China

This book was printed
and bound using a variety of
sustainable manufacturing
processes and materials
including soy-based inks,
acqueous-based varnish, VOC-
and formaldehyde-free glues,
and phthalate-free laminations.
The text is printed in
five colors using offset sheetfed
lithographic printing process
on 157gsm premium matte art
paper with an off-line gloss
acqueous spot varnish applied
to all photographs.

Goff Books makes
a continuous effort to
minimize the overall carbon
footprint of its publications.
As part of this goal,
Goff Books, in association
with Global ReLeaf,
arranges to plant trees to
replace those used in the
manufacturing of the paper
produced for its books.
Global ReLeaf is an
international campaign run
by American Forests,
one of the world's oldest
nonprofit conservation
organizations. Global ReLeaf
is American Forests'
education and action program
that helps individuals,
organizations, agencies,
and corporations improve
the local and global
environment by planting
and caring for trees.

Library of Congress data:
Available upon request

For information
on our distribution,
please visit our website:
www.oroeditions.com